THE KNITTING STITCH MANUAL

THE KNITTING STITCH MANUAL

CASSELL

LESLEY STANFIELD

A QUARTO BOOK

First published in the UK
1992 by Cassell
Villiers House
41/47 Strand
London
WC2N 5JE

**British Library Cataloguing-in-Publication Data. A catalogue
record for this book is available from the British Library.**

ISBN 0-304-34137-1

This book was designed and produced by
Quarto Publishing plc
6 Blundell Street
London N7 9BH

Senior Editor: Honor Head
Art Editor: Anne Fisher
Design: Jane Parker
Photography: Martin Norris
Charts: Jennie Dooge

Art Director: Moira Clinch
Publishing Director: Janet Slingsby

The author would like to send special thanks to
Hilary Underwood and Helen Fraser who helped to knit the
samples and Sue Horan who checked them.

Typeset by En to En, Kent
Manufactured in Singapore by Bright Arts
Printed in Hong Kong by Leefung

CONTENTS

INTRODUCTION

When I began to gather material for this book I realized that my hundreds of old knitting leaflets were a rich source of lost or neglected stitches and that I had a wonderful excuse to browse through them. When recreated the stitch shown sometimes turned out so badly it was easy to see why it had fallen into disuse! However, for every disappointment several lovely stitches emerged from obscurity to be included in this collection.

My own contributions are mostly adaptations of traditional stitch patterns from many countries, an attempt to prove that hand knitting is an evolutionary and not a static art. They reflect my fascination with the inexhaustible variety of effects which can be produced with a pair of knitting needles and a ball of yarn.

The first section of this book is devoted to the simplest formula of all, the combination of knit and purl to make relief stitches ranging from the abstract to the pictorial. The second section contains some of the highly embossed effects which cables offer. Cabling is probably the most versatile technique there is and can be used on its own or with other stitch patterns. The third section includes both bobble and lace stitches which are wonderfully complementary. Scattered or clustered together, bobbles enliven the surface of hand knitting, while lacy stitches have a charm of their own, allowing light to pass through and emphasize their fragility. The final section is a miscellany including many twist stitches, which are a sometimes overlooked method of creating linear textures and cable effects without the use of a third needle.

Charts have been used to explain the stitch patterns because they are more concise and explicit than stitch-by-stitch written instructions, although both are used in the early pages as an aid to readers who are unfamiliar with charted instructions. Learning to work from charts is not difficult if it's taken one step at a time. The book is arranged so that each section runs from easy examples at the beginning to more advanced ones at the end. A knitter with basic skills will quickly gain confidence as the principles of working from charts are understood. The charts are fully explained in a section at the beginning of the book, followed by a list of abbreviations and a glossary of symbols.

Before selecting a stitch and casting on, it's important to remember that knitting is about creating a fabric as well as making decorative patterns. Some hand-knitted fabrics are more stable than others, some are more dense, some are open, some expand and some contract, so it's essential to consider the use that the knitting will be put to when selecting yarn and stitch. Different yarns have been used throughout this book to suggest the characteristics of various stitches but experiment is really the best way to test the suitability of a stitch for a particular purpose. However, don't be inhibited or imagine there are rules that can't be broken. Some mistakes turn out to be happy accidents and many a new stitch pattern is the result of an old one being bungled!

The majority of designs in this book are easy to follow and a large chart may be based on repetition rather than complexity. So don't be afraid to tackle something just because it's large scale or looks complicated.
Have a go and happy knitting!

Lesley Stanfield

KNIT

AND

PURL

STITCHES

CABLE

STITCHES

LACE

AND

BOBBLE

STITCHES

273 274 275 276 277

278 279 280 281 282

283 284 285 286 287

288 289 290 291 292

293 294 295

TWIST

AND

OTHER

STITCHES

296 297 298 299

300 301 302 303

HOW TO USE THE CHARTS

Working from charts has many advantages, the main one being the immediacy with which the relationship between stitches and rows is illustrated. This makes understanding the construction of a stitch pattern and memorising a repeat much easier. It's also an incentive to adapt existing stitches and invent new ones.

As the number of different symbols used in any one stitch pattern is small, they can be learned a few at a time as required. All the symbols have been chosen to be pictorial rather than abstract representations of a stitch or technique.

Chart A

CHART A

● Each square of the chart represents a stitch and each row of squares represents a row of stitches.

● The numbers up the sides of the chart are row numbers and therefore progress from the bottom to the top like the knitted sample.

● All rows which are numbered on the right-hand side of the chart are read from that side and represent right-side rows.

● All rows which are numbered on the left-hand side of the chart are read from that side and represent wrong-side rows. It's useful to get into the habit of reading all charts in this way and it's essential when working stitch patterns which are not symmetrical.

Thus, Chart A reads:

1st row: (right side) k5, p1, k1. (Worked from right to left.)
2nd row: p1, k1, p5. (Worked from left to right.)
3rd row: k4, p1, k2. (Worked from right to left.)
4th row: p2, k1, p4. . . and so on, reading right-side rows from the right and wrong-side rows from the left.

● If a stitch pattern is to be worked in the round with right-side facing, all rows are read from the right-hand side.

CHART B

Each symbol within a square indicates the way a stitch is worked. Initially, it may seem confusing that a blank square represents two stitches – knit on a right-side row and purl on a wrong-side row – and that a dot represents two stitches – purl on

Chart Bi

end of the row) have the cable needle held at the front of the work. Thus, in Chart Ci the symbol represents sl (slip) 2 sts on to cable needle and hold at *back*, k2 then k2 from cable needle. In Chart Cii, the symbol represents sl 2 sts on to cable needle and hold at *front*, k2 then k2 from cable needle.

Chart Ci   Chart Cii

Chart Bii

a right-side row and knit on a wrong-side row. But comparing a knitted sample with its chart reveals the logic of this immediately. The blank squares convey the appearance of the smooth side of the stitch as in stocking stitch, and the dotted squares convey the appearance of the rounded side of the stitch as in reverse stocking stitch (see charts and samples Bi and Bii). All that's needed to know whether a stitch is knit or purl is to know which side of the fabric is being worked.

CHART C

Cable symbols extend over the number of stitches involved in the cable cross, so the cable glossary runs from the smallest cables requiring only two stitches to those requiring nine stitches. As far as possible, the symbols are drawn to look like the resulting cable. In this collection cables are worked on right-side rows only and so it helps to remember that diagonals which slope backwards (i.e. towards the beginning of the row) have the cable needle held at the back of the work and diagonals which slope forwards (i.e. towards the

CHARTS D AND E

To make some charts look more like the resulting cable stitches additional lines have been drawn in. These are merely to help the eye distinguish between one group of stitches and another and do not affect the working of the stitches. In the same way, lines have been used to distinguish one area from another where symbols are very dense and might be difficult to follow.

Chart D   Chart E

These verticals are not worked.

Any exceptional symbols are explained beside the relevant chart.

CHART F

A blocked-out square represents no stitch at all. For example, a stitch lost by decreasing and not compensated for with an increase. These blocked-out areas are not to be included in any stitch count and any loss of vertical alignment of stitches in the chart must be ignored.

Thus, F shows a chart which begins with 5 sts, increases 2 sts on both rows 3 and 5, is worked

19

over 9 sts on rows 6, 7, and 8 before decreasing 2 sts on both rows 9 and 11 to return to 5 sts on row 12.

Chart F

CHART G

• The area of a chart which is unshaded and also has a square bracket underneath indicates a group of stitches forming a repeat.

• A shaded area indicates stitches which are worked at the beginning or end of a row to balance the repeat.

• The number of stitches required for the repeat is given as a "Multiple of . . . sts" and the number of end stitches as "plus . . .".

In Chart G "Multiple of 8 sts plus 1" means cast on a number of stitches divisible by 8 and add 1 more.

Chart G

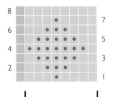

Multiple of 8 sts plus 1.

CHARTS H AND I

An unshaded area underlined by an H-shaped bracket indicates a panel or motif and shaded areas indicate a notional number of stitches to the sides of the pattern area. In a panel all the rows of the chart are repeated. A motif may have an odd number of rows and any number of "background" rows may be worked below and above.

Chart H

Panel of 7 sts.

Chart I

Motif of 7 sts.

GLOSSARY OF SYMBOLS

ABBREVIATIONS

Alt	Alternate.
K	Knit.
Psso	Pass slipped st(s) over.
P	Purl.
RS	Right side.
Skpo	Sl I st knitwise, k I, pass slipped st over.
Sl	Slip.
St(s)	Stitch(es).
Tbl	Through back of loop(s).
Tog	Together.
T2l	Twist 2 sts to left: taking needle behind work, k in back loop of 2nd st on left-hand needle, k in front of Ist st; sl both sts off tog.
T2r	Twist 2 sts to right: k2 tog leaving sts on needle, insert right-hand needle between sts just worked and k Ist st again; sl both sts from needle.
WS	Wrong side.
Yo	Yarn forward and over needle to make a st.

K1 on right-side rows, p1 on wrong-side rows.

P1 on right-side rows, k1 on wrong-side rows.

K1 tbl on right-side rows, p1 tbl on wrong-side rows.

K1 tbl on wrong-side rows.

Sl 1 st purlwise, taking yarn behind work.

Sl 1 st purlwise, taking yarn in front of work.

Yarn forward and over needle to make a st.

Make a st by picking up strand in front of next st and k it in back.

Make a st by picking up strand in front of next st and p it in back.

Increase 1 st by working k in front, then back, of st.

Increase 1 st by working p in back, then front, of st.

Increase 2 sts by working (k1, p1, k1) in st.

Increase 2 sts by working (k1 tbl, k1) in st then insert left-hand needle behind the vertical strand running downwards between the 2 sts just worked and work this strand k1 tbl.

Multiple increase – method given beside chart.

K2 tog on right-side rows, p2 tog on wrong-side rows.

Skpo on right-side rows, p2 tog tbl on wrong-side rows.

P2 tog on right-side rows, k2 tog on wrong-side rows.

P2 tog tbl on right-side rows.

K3 tog.

K3 tog tbl.

P3 tog.

Sl 1 knitwise, k2 tog, psso.

Sl 2 sts as if to work k2 tog; k1, psso.

Cast off 1 st.

St left on right-hand needle after casting off.

Knot: (k1, p1, k1, p1, k1) in st to make 5 sts from 1, then pass 2nd, 3rd, 4th and 5th sts, one at a time, over Ist st.

Large knot: (K1, p1, k1, p1, k1, p1, k1) in st to make 7 sts from 1, pass 2nd, 3rd, 4th, 5th, 6th and 7th sts, one at a time, over Ist st.

Small bobble: (k1, p1, k1, p1, k1) in st to make 5 sts from 1, turn, p5, turn; pass 2nd, 3rd, 4th and 5th sts, one at a time, over Ist st then k in back of this st.

Large bobble: (k1, p1, k1, p1, k1) in st to make 5 sts from 1, turn, p5, turn, k5, turn, p5, turn; pass 2nd, 3rd, 4th and 5th sts over Ist st then k in back of this st.

21

⦿

Purl bobble: (p in front, back, front, back, front) of st to make 5 sts from 1, turn, k5, turn, p5, turn, k5, turn; pass 2nd, 3rd, 4th and 5th sts, one at a time, over 1st st then k in back of this st.

▬

Wide bobble: [k2, turn, p2, turn] twice, [k next st tog with corresponding st of 1st row of bobble] twice.

▭▭▭▭

Sl 3 sts on to cable needle, wind yarn anti-clockwise around base of sts 8 times, ending with yarn at back of work, sl sts on to right-hand needle.

▭▭▭▭▭▭

Sl 4 sts on to cable needle, wind yarn anti-clockwise around base of sts 4 times, ending with yarn at back of work, sl sts on to right-hand needle.

▭▭▭▭▭▭▭

Sl 5 sts on to cable needle, wind yarn anti-clockwise around base of sts 4 times, ending with yarn at back of work, sl sts on to right-hand needle.

▭▭▭▭▭▭▭▭

Sl 6 sts on to cable needle, wind yarn anti-clockwise around base of sts 4 times, ending with yarn at back of work, sl sts on to right-hand needle.

▦▦▦▦▦▦▦▦▦▦▦

Sl 10 sts on to cable needle, wind yarn anti-clockwise around base of sts 4 times, ending with yarn at back of work, sl sts on to right-hand needle.

■

No stitch.

◰

Twist 2 sts to right: k2 tog, leaving sts on needle, insert right-hand needle between sts just worked and k 1st st again; sl both sts off tog.

◰

Twist 2 sts to left: taking needle behind work, k in back loop of 2nd st on left-hand needle, k in front of 1st st; sl both sts off tog.

◰

Purl twist to right: taking needle to front of work, k 2nd st on left-hand needle, p 1st st; sl both sts off tog.

◰

Purl twist to left: taking needle behind work, p in back of 2nd st on left-hand needle, k in front of 1st st; sl both sts off tog.

◰

Twist 3 sts: taking needle to front of work, k 3rd st on left-hand needle, then 2nd st, then 1st st; sl all sts off tog.

CABLES

⟋⟋

Sl 1 st on to cable needle and hold at back, k1 then k1 from cable needle.

⟍⟍

Sl 1 st on to cable needle and hold at front, k1 then k1 from cable needle.

⟋⟋

Sl 1 st on to cable needle and hold at back, k1 then p1 from cable needle.

⟍◉

Sl 1 st on to cable needle and hold at front, p1 then k1 from cable needle.

⟋⟋⟋

Sl 2 sts on to cable needle and hold at back, k1 then k2 from cable needle.

Sl 1 st on to cable needle and hold at front, k2 then k1 from cable needle.

Sl 2 sts on to cable needle and hold at back, k1 then p2 from cable needle.

Sl 1 st on to cable needle and hold at front, p2 then k1 from cable needle.

Sl 2 sts on to cable needle and hold at back, k1, sl last st from cable needle back on to left-hand needle and p this st then k1 from cable needle.

Sl 1 st on to cable needle and hold at front, k1, p1 then k1 from cable needle.

Sl 1 st on to cable needle and hold at back, k2 then k1 from cable needle.

Sl 2 sts on to cable needle and hold at front, k1 then k2 from cable needle.

Sl 1 st on to cable needle and hold at back, k2 then p1 from cable needle.

Sl 2 sts on to cable needle and hold at front, p1 then k2 from cable needle.

Sl 1 st on to cable needle and hold at back, t 2 r then p1 from cable needle.

Sl 2 sts on to cable needle and hold at front, p1 then t 2 r from cable needle.

Sl 2 sts on to cable needle and hold at back, k2 then k2 from cable needle.

Sl 2 sts on to cable needle and hold at front, k2 then k2 from cable needle.

Sl 2 sts on to cable needle and hold at back, k2 then p2 from cable needle.

Sl 2 sts on to cable needle and hold at front, p2 then k2 from cable needle.

Sl 1 st on to cable needle and hold at back, k3 then p1 from cable needle.

Sl 3 sts on to cable needle and hold at front, p1 then k3 from cable needle.

Sl 3 sts on to cable needle and hold at back, k2, sl last st from cable needle back on to left-hand needle and k this st then k2 from cable needle.

Sl 2 sts on to 1st cable needle and hold at front, sl 1 st on to 2nd cable needle and hold at back, k2; k1 from 2nd cable needle then k2 from 1st cable needle.

Sl 3 sts on to cable needle and hold at back, k2, sl last st from cable needle back on to left-hand needle and p this st then k2 from cable needle.

Sl 2 sts on to 1st cable needle and hold at front, sl 1 st on to 2nd cable needle and hold at back, k2; p1 from 2nd cable needle then k2 from 1st cable needle.

Sl 1 st on to 1st cable needle and hold at front, sl 3 sts on to 2nd cable needle and hold at back, k1; p3 from 2nd cable needle then k1 from 1st cable needle.

Sl 2 sts on to cable needle and hold at back, k3 then p2 from cable needle.

Sl 3 sts on to cable needle and hold at front, p2 then k3 from cable needle.

Sl 1 st on to cable needle and hold at back, t 2 r, t 2 l then k1 from cable needle.

Sl 4 sts on to cable needle and hold at front, k1 then t 2 r, t 2 l from cable needle.

Sl 1 st on to cable needle and hold at back, t 2 r, t 2 l then p1 from cable needle.

Sl 4 sts on to cable needle and hold at front, p1 then t 2 r, t 2 l from cable needle.

Sl 1 st on to cable needle and hold at back, t 2 l, t 2 r then p1 from cable needle.

Sl 4 sts on to cable needle and hold at front, p1 then t 2 l, t 2 r from cable needle.

Sl 3 sts on to cable needle and hold at back, k3 then k3 from cable needle.

Sl 3 sts on to cable needle and hold at front, k3 then k3 from cable needle.

Sl 4 sts on to cable needle and hold at back, k2, sl last 2 sts from cable needle back on to left-hand needle and p these 2 sts then k2 from cable needle.

Sl 2 sts on to 1st cable needle and hold at front, sl 2 sts on to 2nd cable needle and hold at back, k2; p2 from 2nd cable needle then k2 from 1st cable needle.

Sl 4 sts on to cable needle and hold at back, k3, sl last st from cable needle back on to left-hand needle and k this st then k3 from cable needle.

Sl 4 sts on to cable needle and hold at back, k3, sl last st from cable needle back on to left-hand needle and p this st then k3 from cable needle.

Sl 4 sts on to cable needle and hold at back, k4 then k4 from cable needle.

Sl 4 sts on to cable needle and hold at front, k4 then k4 from cable needle.

Sl 5 sts on to cable needle and hold at back, k4 then k5 from cable needle.

Sl 4 sts on to cable needle and hold at back, k5 then k4 from cable needle.

KNIT AND PURL STITCHES

Knit and purl stitches are the basis of all knitting. On their own they offer a tremendous number of possibilities. The smoothness of the "knit" side of the stitch and the roundness of the "purl" side can be contrasted to make textures as varied as moss stitch and brocade. The stitches can be aligned vertically to make ribs or horizontally to make ridges. In turn, these can be combined to make brick patterns and basket weaves.

The very simplest knit and purl textures are sometimes overlooked, but a sweater banded with many small-repeat, grainy stitches would be very attractive. Fishermen's Guernseys decorated with knit and purl geometrics are enduring classics. Whatever the design, it's advisable to use a round, firm yarn and a close tension to emphasize the contrast between smooth and raised stitches.

Multiple of 4 sts plus 1.

1st row: (right side) k.
2nd row: p.
3rd row: * k1, p3; repeat from * to last st, k1.
4th row: p.
Repeat rows 1-4.

Multiple of 5 sts plus 2.

1st row: (right side) * k2, p3; repeat from * to last 2 sts, k2.
2nd row: p.
Repeat rows 1 and 2.

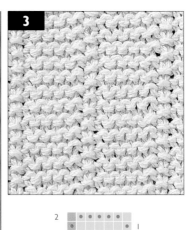

Multiple of 6 sts plus 1.
This stitch is reversible.

1st row: (right side) * p1, k5; repeat from * to last st, p1.
2nd row: p1, * k5, p1; repeat from * to end.
Repeat rows 1 and 2.

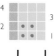

Multiple of 3 sts plus 1.

1st row: (right side) * k1, p2; repeat from * to last st, k1.
2nd row: p1, * k2, p1; repeat from * to end.
3rd row: k.
4th row: p.
Repeat rows 1-4.

Multiple of 4 sts plus 2.

1st row: (right side) p.
2nd row: k.
3rd row: * k2, p2; repeat from * to last 2 sts, k2.
4th row: p2, * k2, p2; repeat from * to end.
Repeat rows 1-4.

Multiple of 4 sts plus 1.

1st row: (right side) * k1, p3; repeat from * to last st, k1.
2nd row: p.
3rd row: * p2, k1, p1; repeat from * to last st, p1.
4th row: p.
Repeat rows 1-4.

Multiple of 10 sts plus 6.

Ist row: (right side) * p6, k4; repeat from * to last 6 sts, p6.
2nd row: p.
3rd row: * p1, k4, p5; repeat from * to last 6 sts, p1, k4, p1.
4th row: p.
Repeat rows 1-4.

Multiple of 6 sts plus 3.
This stitch is reversible.

Ist row: (right side) * p1, k1; repeat from * to last st, p1.
2nd row: k3, * p3, k3; repeat from * to end.
Repeat rows 1 and 2.

Multiple of 6 sts plus 3.

Ist row: (right side) * p1, k1, p4; repeat from * to last 3 sts, p1, k1, p1.
2nd row: k1, p1, k1, * p3, k1, p1, k1; repeat from * to end.
3rd row: * p3, k3; repeat from * to last 3 sts, p3.
4th row: k1, p1, k1, * p3, k1, p1, k1; repeat from * to end.
Repeat rows 1-4.

Multiple of 8 sts plus 5.

Ist row: (right side) * p2, k1, p2, k3; repeat from * to last 5 sts, p2, k1, p2.
2nd row: k5, * k1, p1, k6; repeat from * to end.
Repeat rows 1 and 2.

11

12

13

Multiple of 6 sts plus 3.

1st and 3rd rows: (right side) *
k3, p1, k1, p1; repeat from * to
last 3 sts, k3.
2nd row: p3, * k3, p3; repeat
from * to end.
4th row: p.
5th and 7th rows: * p1, k1, p1,
k3; repeat from * to last 3 sts,
p1, k1, p1.
6th row: k3, * p3, k3; repeat
from * to end.
8th row: p.
Repeat rows 1-8.

Multiple of 4 sts plus 3.

1st row: (right side) * p1, k1,
p2; repeat from * to last 3 sts,
p1, k1, p1.
2nd row: k1, p1, k1, * k2, p1, k1;
repeat from * to end.
3rd row: * p1, k1; repeat from
* to last st, p1.
4th row: k1, * p1, k1; repeat
from * to end.
5th row: * p3, k1; repeat from
* to last 3 sts, p3.
6th row: k3, * p1, k3; repeat
from * to end.
7th row: as 3rd row.
8th row: as 4th row.
Repeat rows 1-8.

Multiple of 2 sts plus 1.

1st and 3rd rows: (right side)
k.
2nd and 4th rows: p.
5th row: * k1, p1; repeat from
* to last st, k1.
6th row: p1, * k1, p1; repeat
from * to end.
Repeat rows 1-6.

14

15

16

Multiple of 6 sts plus 4.

1st and 3rd rows: (right side)
* k1, p2, k3; repeat from * to
last 4 sts, k1, p2, k1.
2nd and alt rows: p.
5th and 7th rows: * k4, p2;
repeat from * to last 4 sts, k4.
8th row: p.
Repeat rows 1-8.

Multiple of 8 sts plus 1.

1st, 3rd, 5th and 7th rows:
(right side) * k2, p1, k3, p1, k1;
repeat from * to last st, k1.
2nd, 4th and 6th rows: p1,
* p1, k5, p2; repeat from * to
end.
8th and 10th rows: k1, * k2,
p3, k3; repeat from * to end.
9th and 11th rows: * k2, p1,
k3, p1, k1; repeat from * to last
st, k1.
12th row: as 8th row.
Repeat rows 1-12.

Multiple of 8 sts plus 2.

1st row: (right side) * k2, p6;
repeat from * to last 2 sts, k2.
2nd row: p2, * k6, p2; repeat
from * to end.
3rd row: k.
4th row: k2, * k2, p2, k4;
repeat from * to end.
5th row: * p4, k2, p2; repeat
from * to last 2 sts, p2.
6th row: p.
Repeat rows 1-6.

17

18

Multiple of 11 sts.

1st row: (right side) * p3, [k1, p3] twice; repeat from * to end.
2nd row: * k3, [p1, k3] twice; repeat from * to end.
3rd row: k.
4th row: * k5, p1, k5; repeat from * to end.
5th row: * p5, k1, p5; repeat from * to end.
6th row: p.
Repeat rows 1-6.

Multiple of 12 sts plus 8.

1st row: (right side) * p8, k4; repeat from * to last 8 sts, p8.
2nd row: k8, * p4, k8; repeat from * to end.
3rd row: * p2, k4, p6; repeat from * to last 8 sts, p2, k4, p2.
4th row: k2, p4, k2, * k6, p4, k2; repeat from * to end.
Repeat rows 1-4.

19

20

Multiple of 9 sts plus 2.

1st row: (right side) * k2, p2, k3, p2; repeat from * to last 2 sts, k2.
2nd row: p.
3rd row: * k2, p7; repeat from * to last 2 sts, k2.
4th row: p.
Repeat rows 1-4.

Multiple of 8 sts plus 4.
This stitch is reversible.

1st row: (right side) * k4, p4; repeat from * to last 4 sts, k4.
2nd and alt rows: k all k sts and p all p sts as they appear.
3rd row: p.
5th row: as 1st row.
7th row: k.
8th row: as 2nd row.
Repeat rows 1-8.

21

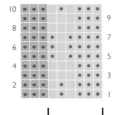

Multiple of 2 sts plus 1.

23

Multiple of 12 sts plus 6.

22

Multiple of 6 sts plus 3.

24

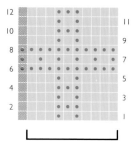

25

Multiple of 10 sts plus 1.

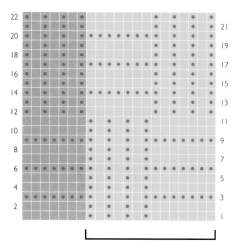

Multiple of 14 sts plus 7.

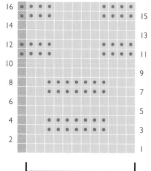

26

Multiple of 12 sts plus 1.

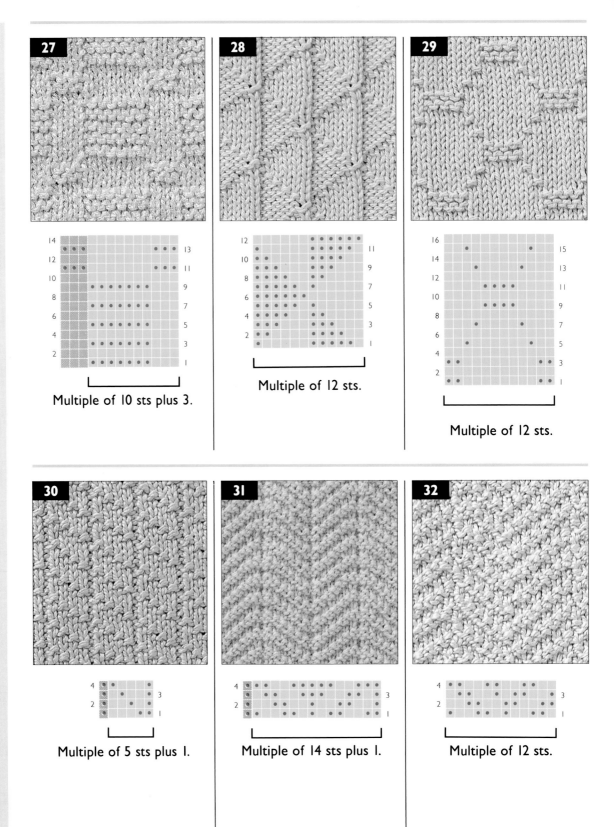

27

Multiple of 10 sts plus 3.

28

Multiple of 12 sts.

29

Multiple of 12 sts.

30

Multiple of 5 sts plus 1.

31

Multiple of 14 sts plus 1.

32

Multiple of 12 sts.

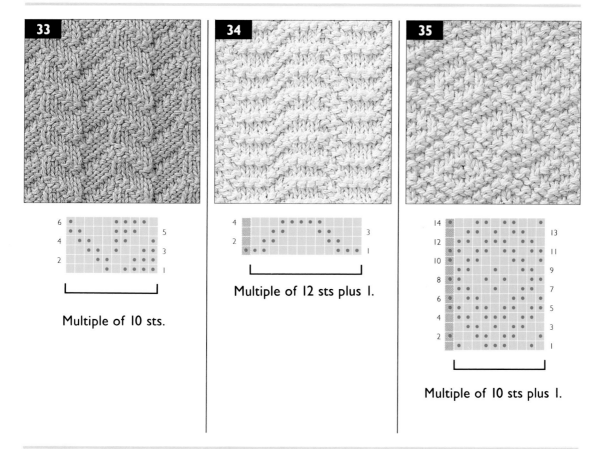

33

Multiple of 10 sts.

34

Multiple of 12 sts plus 1.

35

Multiple of 10 sts plus 1.

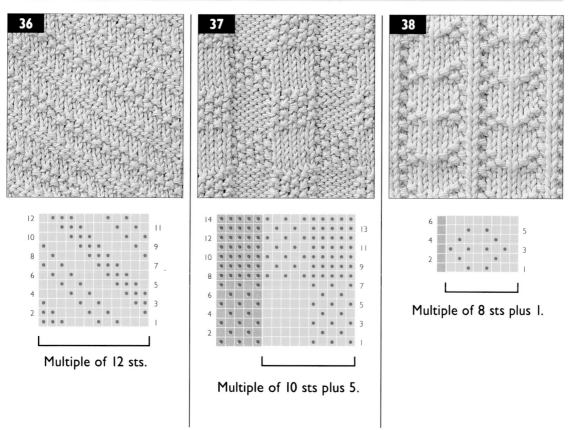

36

Multiple of 12 sts.

37

Multiple of 10 sts plus 5.

38

Multiple of 8 sts plus 1.

39

Multiple of 10 sts plus 1.

40

Multiple of 8 sts plus 5.

41

Multiple of 6 sts plus 2.

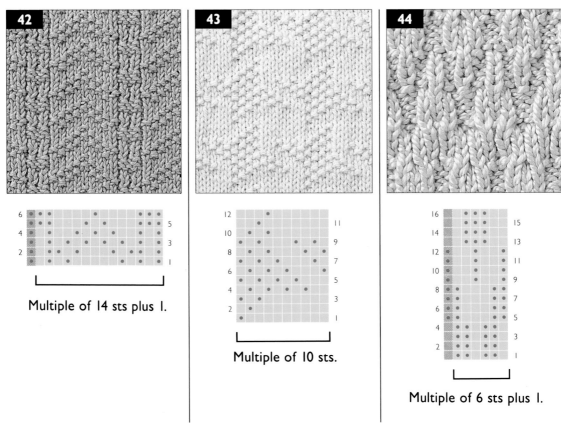

42

Multiple of 14 sts plus 1.

43

Multiple of 10 sts.

44

Multiple of 6 sts plus 1.

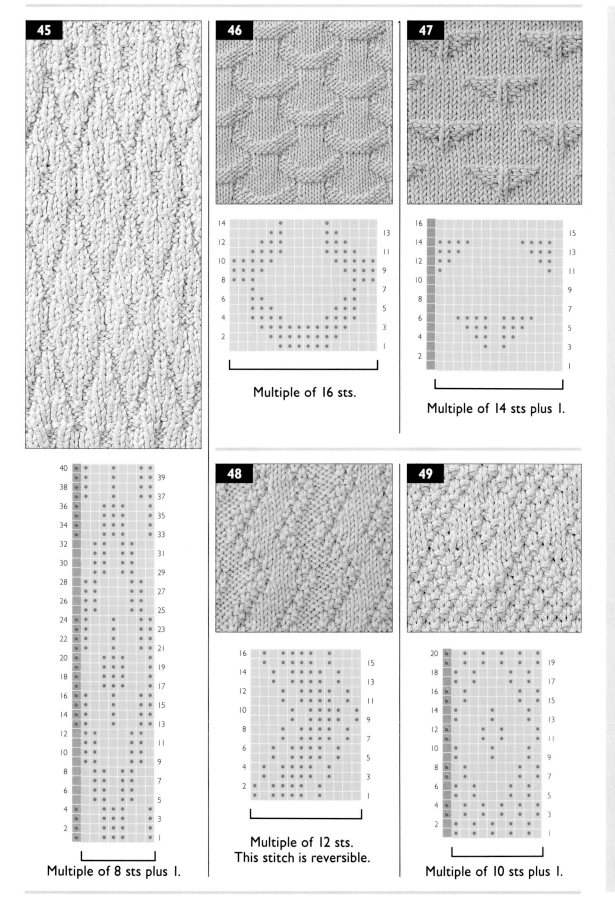

45

46

Multiple of 16 sts.

47

Multiple of 14 sts plus 1.

Multiple of 8 sts plus 1.

48

Multiple of 12 sts.
This stitch is reversible.

49

Multiple of 10 sts plus 1.

50

51

Multiple of 10 sts.

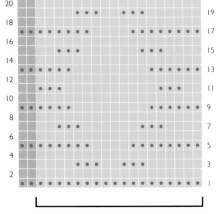

Multiple of 18 sts plus 2.

52

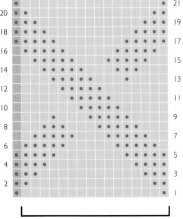

Multiple of 16 sts plus 1.

53

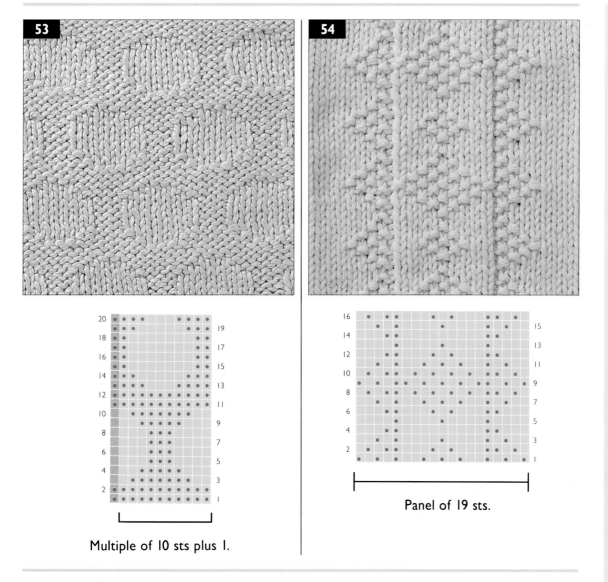

Multiple of 10 sts plus 1.

54

Panel of 19 sts.

55

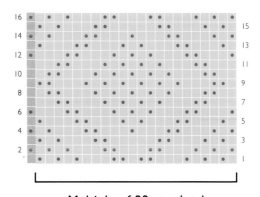

Multiple of 22 sts plus 1.

56

57

Multiple of 18 sts plus 1.

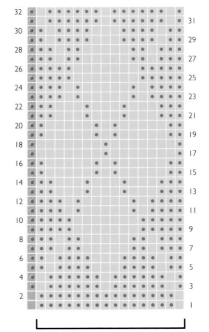

Multiple of 16 sts plus 1.

58

59

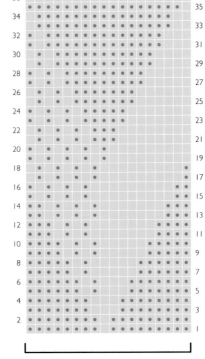

Multiple of 12 sts.
This stitch is reversible.

Multiple of 18 sts.

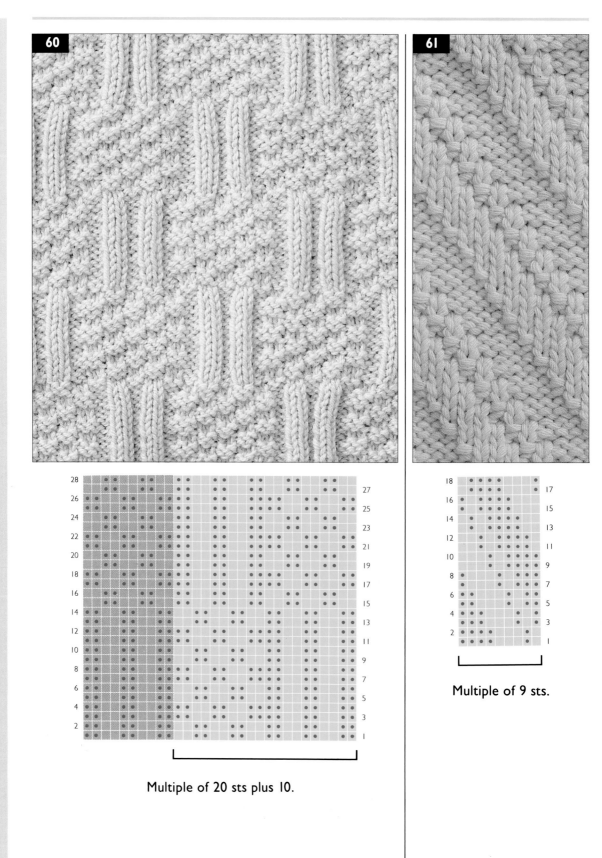

60

61

Multiple of 20 sts plus 10.

Multiple of 9 sts.

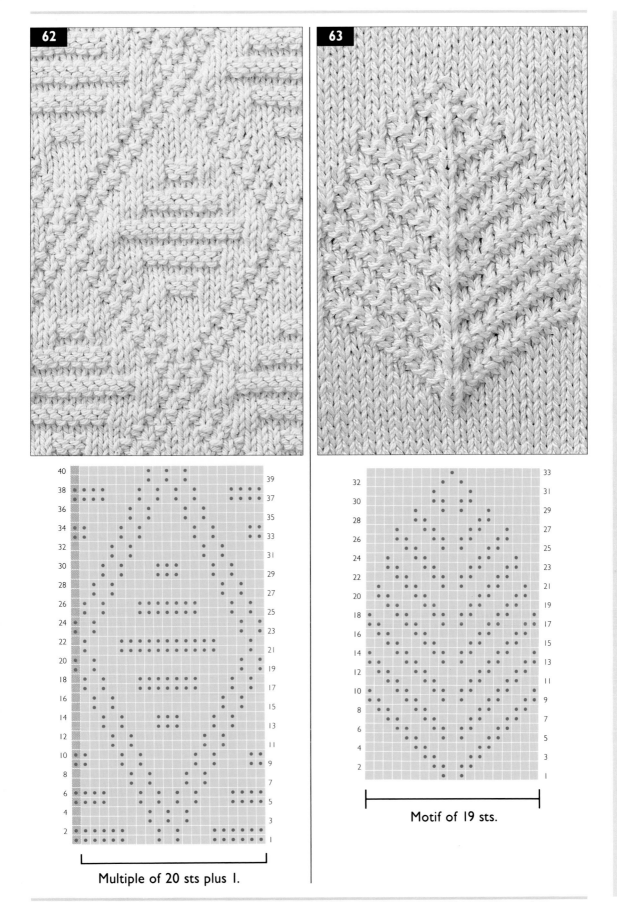

62

63

Multiple of 20 sts plus 1.

Motif of 19 sts.

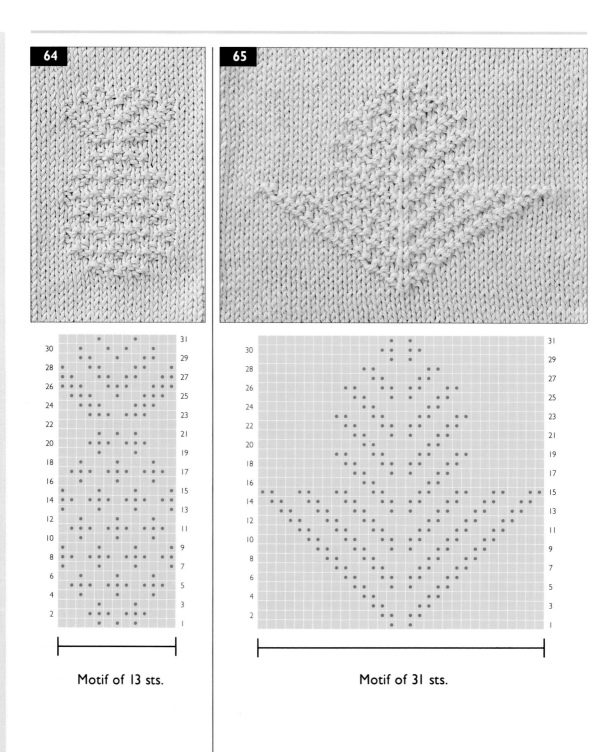

Motif of 13 sts.

Motif of 31 sts.

66

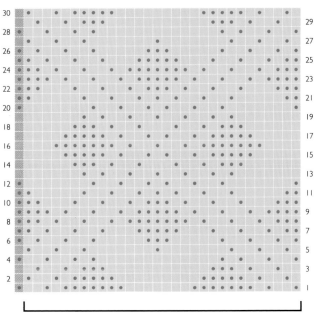

Multiple of 30 sts plus 1.

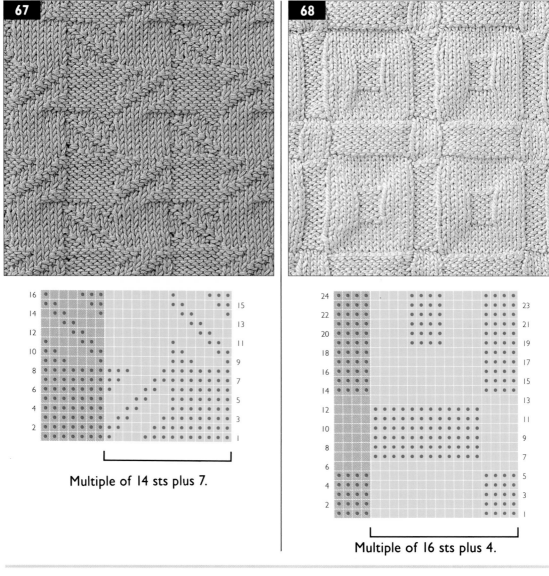

67

Multiple of 14 sts plus 7.

68

Multiple of 16 sts plus 4.

69

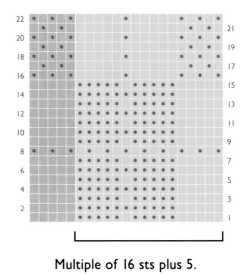

Multiple of 16 sts plus 5.

70

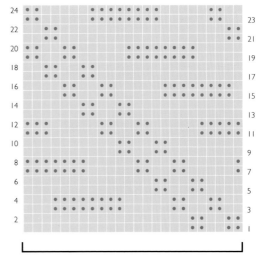

Multiple of 24 sts.

71

Motif of 61 sts.

Multiple of 54 sts plus 1.

72

CABLE STITCHES

Cables are stitches that look like twisted ropes, interwoven plaits and criss-cross trellises and which seem so complicated to the uninitiated. But the principle is simple: making a cable is merely working stitches, or groups of stitches, out of sequence. A cable needle (a short, double-pointed needle) is used to hold the first stitch(es) to the front or back while working the following stitch(es), the knitting is then resumed from the cable needle. Cables are usually worked in stocking stitch on a plain or textured ground but they look particularly rich when they themselves are textured.

As well as raising the surface, cables contract the knitted fabric, so it's usually a good idea to work increases into the base of a cable panel or motif and decreases into the top to prevent flaring below and above. Their density makes cables ideal for outdoor wear.

73

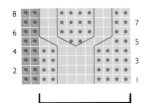

Multiple of 10 sts plus 2.

74

Multiple of 12 sts.

75

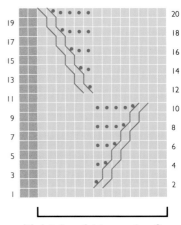

Multiple of 14 sts plus 2.

76

Panel of 8 sts.

77

Panel of 12 sts.

78

Panel of 12 sts.

Sl 4 sts on to cable needle and hold at front, sl 4 sts on to 2nd cable needle and hold at back, k4, then k4 from 2nd cable needle, then k4 from 1st cable needle.

53

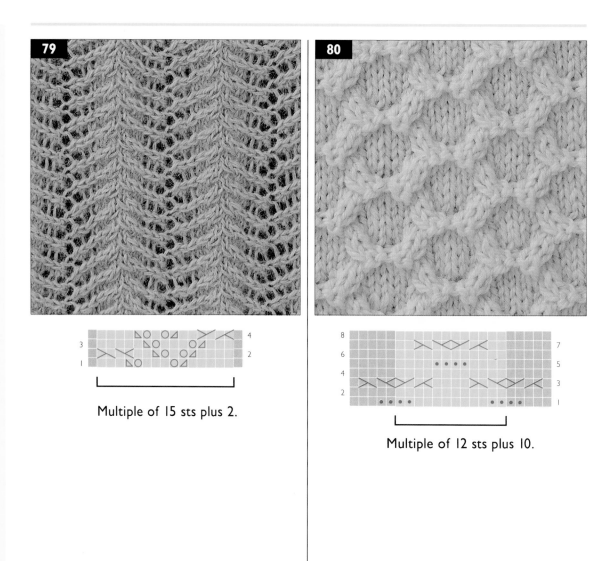

79

Multiple of 15 sts plus 2.

80

Multiple of 12 sts plus 10.

81

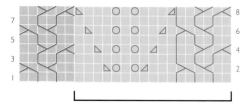

Multiple of 17 sts plus 6.

82

83

Panel of 12 sts.

Motif of 11 sts.

Sl 3 sts on to cable needle and hold at back, k2 then k3 from cable needle.

Sl 2 sts on to cable needle and hold at front, k3 then k2 from cable needle.

Sl 3 sts on to cable needle and hold at back, p1, k1, p1 then k3 from cable needle.

Sl 3 sts on to cable needle and hold at front, k3 then k1, p1, k1 from cable needle.

Sl 3 sts on to cable needle and hold at back, k3 then p1, k1, p1 from cable needle.

Sl 3 sts on to cable needle and hold at front, k1, p1, k1 then k3 from cable needle.

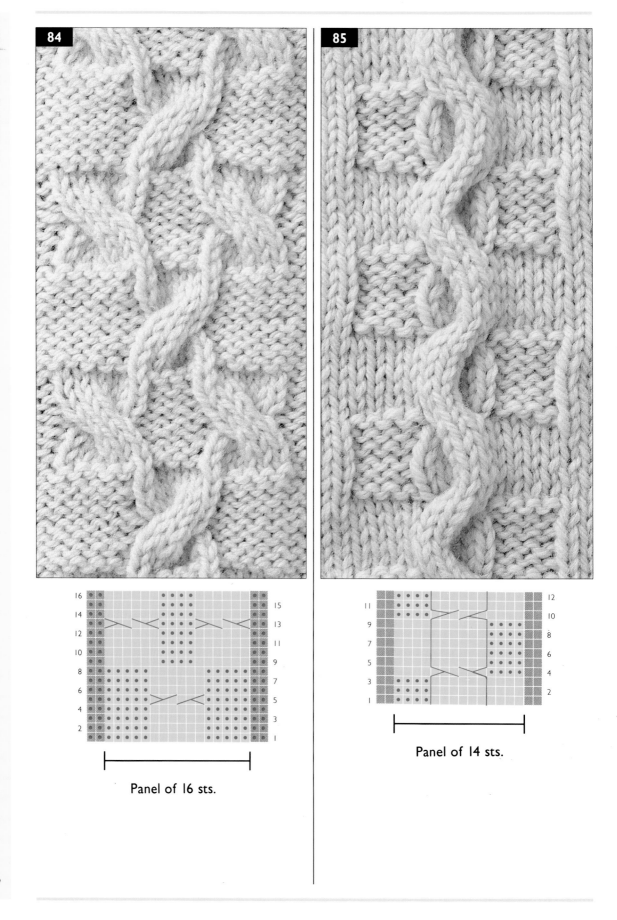

84

85

Panel of 16 sts.

Panel of 14 sts.

86

87

Multiple of 16 sts plus 4.

Panel of 4 sts.

88

Multiple of 18 sts plus 10.

Sl 3 sts on to cable needle and hold at back, k1 then k3 from cable needle, sl 1 st on to cable needle and hold at front, k3 then k1 from cable needle.

89

Panel of 8 sts.

SI 2 sts on to cable needle and hold at front, k4 then k2 from cable needle.

SI 2 sts on to cable needle and hold at front, k6 then k2 from cable needle.

90

Panel of 9 sts.

Multiple of 23 sts plus 11.

Panel of 6 sts.

93

94

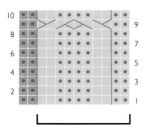

Multiple of 10 sts plus 2.

Panel of 17 sts.

Sl next 2 sts on to cable needle and hold at front, k2 then p2 from cable needle.

Sl next 2 sts on to cable needle and hold at back, p2 then k2 from cable needle.

CABLE STITCHES

95

96

Panel of 12 sts.

Panel of 19 sts.

Panel of 15 sts.

Multiple of 11 sts.

99

100

Panel of 14 sts.

Multiple of 12 sts plus 13.

101

Panel of 10 sts.

Sl 3 sts on to cable needle and hold at back, k2 then p2, k1 from cable needle.

Sl 2 sts on to cable needle and hold at front, k1, p2 then k2 from cable needle.

Sl 2 sts on to cable needle and hold at front, k3 then k2 from cable needle.

Sl 3 sts on to cable needle and hold at back, k2 then k3 from cable needle.

102

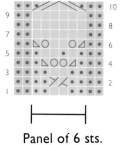

Panel of 6 sts.

CABLE STITCHES

103

104

105

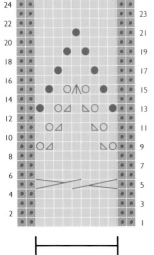

24
22
20
18
16
14
12
10
8
6
4
2

23
21
19
17
15
13
11
9
7
5
3
1

Panel of 9 sts.

8
6
4
2

7
5
3
1

Multiple of 8 sts plus 2.

Sl 3 sts on to cable needle
and hold at front, k1, p2
then k3 from cable needle.

12
11
10
9
8
7
6
5
4
3
2
1

Panel of 12 sts.

Sl 2 sts on to cable needle
and hold at front, sl next 4
sts on to 2nd cable needle
and hold at back, k2, then k4
from 2nd cable needle, then
k2 from 1st cable needle.

66

106

Multiple of 20 sts plus 21.

107

108

Panel of 14 sts.

Panel of 21 sts.

Sl next 3 sts on to cable needle and hold at back, p1, k2 then p3 from cable needle.

Sl next 3 sts on to cable needle and hold at front, p3 then k2, p1 from cable needle.

109

110

Panel of 18 sts.

Multiple of 18 sts.

Sl 3 sts on to cable needle
and hold at front, k2 then k3
from cable needle.

Sl 2 sts on to cable needle
and hold at back, k3 then k2
from cable needle.

Panel of 8 sts.

Motif of 9 sts.

Panel of 11 sts.

Sl next 6 sts on to cable needle and hold at back, k1, p1, k1, then work 6 sts from cable needle: [p1, k1] 3 times.

CABLE STITCHES

Multiple of 6 sts plus 1.

SI 1 st on to cable needle
and hold at front, sl next 3
sts on to 2nd cable needle
and hold at back, k1, then p3
from 2nd cable needle, then
k1 from 1st cable needle.

Panel of 12 sts.

Panel of 16 sts.

71

117

Panel of 10 sts.

118

Panel of 10 sts.

Sl next 2 sts on to cable needle and hold at front, p2, k2 then k2 from cable needle.

Sl next 4 sts on to cable needle and hold at back, k2 then p4 from cable needle.

119

Panel of 30 sts.

120

Panel of 12 sts.

121

Multiple of 24 sts plus 14.

122

Panel of 22 sts.

123

Panel of 14 sts.

124

Panel of 35 sts.

SI next 5 sts on to cable
needle and hold at back, p5
then work k2, p1, k2 from
cable needle.

125

126

Multiple of 12 sts plus 4.

Panel of 9 sts.

Sl 6 sts on to cable needle and hold at back, k3, sl last 3 sts from cable needle back on to left-hand needle, k3 then k3 sts from cable needle.

Sl 3 sts on to 1st cable needle and hold at back, sl next 3 sts on to 2nd cable needle and hold at front, k3, k3 from 2nd cable needle, k3 from 1st cable needle.

127

Panel of 30 sts.

128

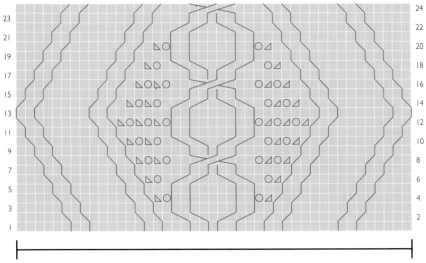

Panel of 43 sts.

129

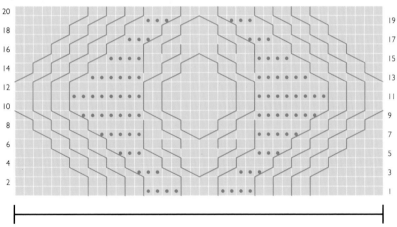

Panel of 40 sts.

130

Panel of 9 sts.

Skpo, k1, k2 tog, to make 3 sts from 5.

P5 on WS rows, k5 on RS rows.

(K1, yo, k1, yo, k1) in st to make 5 sts from 1.

3

P3.

Panel of 28 sts.

Panel of 7 sts.

Multiple of 24 sts plus 12.

Panel of 23 sts.

Motif of 12 sts.

136

Panel of 8 sts.

137

Panel of 15 sts.

138

139

Multiple of 26 sts plus 1.

Panel of 10 sts.

Motif of 19 sts.

Motif of 19 sts.

142

Panel of 19 sts.

143

Panel of 23 sts.

144

145

39 37 35 33 31 29 27 25 23 21 19 17 15 13 11 9 7 5 3 1

40 38 36 34 32 30 28 26 24 22 20 18 16 14 12 10 8 6 4 2

Panel of 11 sts.

26 24 22 20 18 16 14 12 10 8 6 4 2

27 25 23 21 19 17 15 13 11 9 7 5 3 1

Motif of 13 sts.

$\vee$

(K1, yo, k1, yo, k1) to make 5 sts from 1.

5

P5 on WS rows, k5 on RS rows.

$\wedge$

Skpo, k1, k2 tog to make 3 sts from 5.

3

P3.

Sl 2 sts on to cable needle and hold at back, k1 then p1, k1 from cable needle.

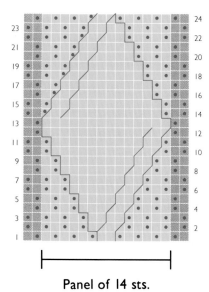

23 24
21 22
19 20
17 18
15 16
13 14
11 12
9   10
7   8
5   6
3   4
1   2

Panel of 14 sts.

146

147

Panel of 12 sts.

148

Panel of 10 sts.

31 32
29 30
27 28
25 26
23 24
21 22
19 20
17 18
15 16
13 14
11 12
9   10
7   8
5   6
3   4
1   2

Panel of 24 sts.

Sl 4 sts on to cable needle and hold at back, k2 then k4 from cable needle.

Sl 2 sts on to cable needle and hold at front, k4 then k2 from cable needle.

Sl 4 sts on to cable needle and hold at back, k2 then work k2, p2 from cable needle.

Sl 2 sts on to cable needle and hold at front, p2, k2 then k2 from cable needle.

149

150

Panel of 11 sts.

151

Multiple of 12 sts.

152

Panel of 20 sts.

153

Multiple of 16 sts plus 4.

Multiple of 10 sts plus 10.

Panel of 16 sts.

156

157

25
23
21
19
17
15
13
11
9
7
5
3
1

26
24
22
20
18
16
14
12
10
8
6
4
2

Panel of 20 sts.

27
25
23
21
19
17
15
13
11
9
7
5
3
1

28
26
24
22
20
18
16
14
12
10
8
6
4
2

Panel of 16 sts.

158

Panel of 27 sts.

159

SI next 3 sts on to cable needle and hold at back, k3 then p3 from cable needle.

SI next 3 sts on to cable needle and hold at front, p3 then k3 from cable needle.

SI next 6 sts on to cable needle and hold at back, k3, sI last 3 sts from cable needle to left-hand needle, p3 then k3 remaining sts from cable needle.

Panel of 5 sts.
All k sts of cables are worked tbl.

160

Panel of 9 sts.

Sl 3 sts on to 1st cable needle and hold at back, sl next 3 sts on to 2nd cable needle and hold at front, k1 tbl, p1, k1 tbl, then work sts from 2nd cable needle p1, k1 tbl, p1, then work sts from 1st cable needle k1 tbl, p1, k1 tbl.

161

162

Panel of 25 sts.

Panel of 15 sts.
All k sts of cables are worked tbl.

163

Panel of 15 sts.

Sl 1 st on to cable needle and hold at back, k1 tbl, [p1, k1 tbl] twice, then p1 from cable needle.

Sl 5 sts on to cable needle and hold at front, p1, then work k1 tbl, [p1, k1 tbl] twice from cable needle.

Sl 6 sts on to cable needle and hold at back, k1 tbl, [p1, k1 tbl] twice, then work sts from cable needle [p1, k1 tbl] 3 times.

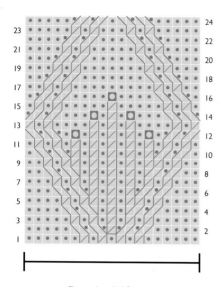

Panel of 19 sts.
All k sts of cables are worked tbl.

165

Panel of 16 sts.

Sl 2 sts on to cable needle and hold at back, K2 then p1, k1 tbl from cable needle.

Sl 2 sts on to cable needle and hold at front, k1 tbl, p1 then k 2 sts from cable needle.

Panel of 12 sts.

166

167

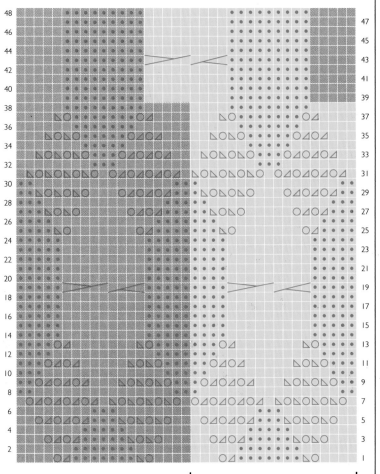

Multiple of 18 sts plus 19.

168

Motif of 13 sts.

Multiple of 12 sts plus 14.

170

171

Panel of 17 sts.

Sl next 3 sts on to cable
needle and hold at back, k4
then k3 from cable needle.

Multiple of 12 sts plus 14.

Panel of 32 sts.

Motif of 27 sts.

174

Panel of 31 sts.

175

176

Panel of 17 sts.

Panel of 19 sts.

177

Multiple of 13 sts plus 13.

178

SI 6 sts on to cable needle and hold at back, k2, p1, k2 then work sts from cable needle [p1, k2] twice.

✳

Drop k st from needle to make a ladder, then work yo. (Ladder will stop at previous yo.)

Note that only rows 1-24 are repeated, foundation row is not. On last row make appropriate ladders before casting off.

Multiple of 26 sts plus 15.

179

Panel of 17 sts.

180

Panel of 41 sts.

181

Panel of 50 sts.

182

Motif of 22 sts.

Multiple of 14 sts plus 15.

184

Panel of 90 sts.

LACE AND BOBBLE STITCHES

Both lace and bobble stitches are very compatible with cables and feature in the previous section. Here, I have used them together and separately so that round, three-dimensional bobbles complement round, open eyelets.

There are many ways of making bobbles but the basic principle I have used is that one stitch is increased into several times, the newly-formed group of stitches is then worked before the increased stitches are passed over the first one, which is worked again to "anchor" it. This gives a firm, round bobble without the tendency to disappear to the wrong side of the knitting. Single eyelets are made by decreasing one stitch and compensating for this with a yarn-over increase. Double eyelets are made by working two decreases with a double yarn over between. They can both be used to form an all-over lacy fabric or to define a pattern on a solid ground.

Lace stitches are usually better worked on a largish needle and in a yarn which can be blocked (that is, shaped and pinned out) and thoroughly pressed.

185

2 [chart]

Multiple of 6 sts plus 4.

186

8
6
4
2

7
5
3
1

[chart]

Multiple of 5 sts plus 3.

187

4
2

3
1

[chart]

Multiple of 5 sts plus 3.

188

4
2

3
1

[chart]

Multiple of 14 sts plus 1.

189

2 [chart] 1

Multiple of 4 sts plus 2.

190

4
2

3
1

[chart]

Multiple of 6 sts plus 5.

K4 tog.

K4 tog tbl.

191

192

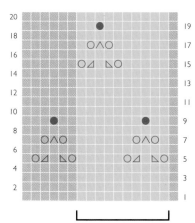

Multiple of 10 sts plus 7.

Panel of 23 sts.

●

(k1, yo, k1, yo, k1) in st to
make 5 sts from 1, turn, p5,
turn, k3, k2 tog, pass 3 sts,
one at a time, over k2 tog.

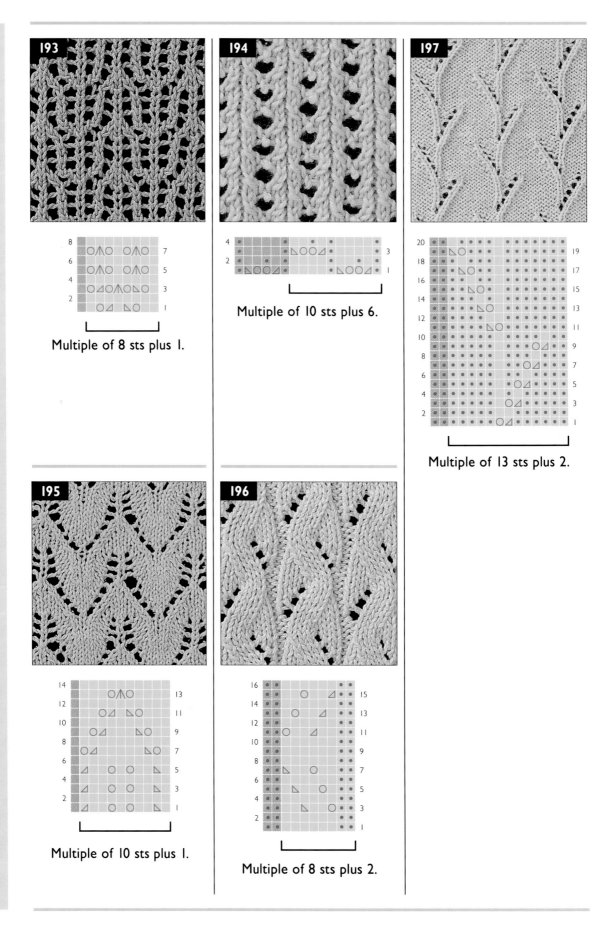

193

8
7 O∧O   O∧O
6
5 O∧O   O∧O
4
3 O⊿O∧O⊿O
2
1 O⊿ ⊿O

Multiple of 8 sts plus 1.

194

4
3 ⊾OO⊿ ●
2
1 ⊾⊿OO∧⊿ ●   ⊾OO⊿

Multiple of 10 sts plus 6.

197

20
19 ⊿O
18
17
16 ⊾O
15
14
13
12 ⊿O
11
10
9 O⊿
8
7 O⊿
6
5 O⊿
4
3 O⊿
2
1 O⊿

Multiple of 13 sts plus 2.

195

14
13   O∧O
12
11   O⊿   ⊾O
10
9 O⊿   ⊾O
8
7 O⊿   ⊾O
6
5 ⊿ O O ⊾
4
3 ⊿ O O ⊾
2
1 ⊿ O O   ⊾

Multiple of 10 sts plus 1.

196

16
15   O   ⊿ ●●
14
13   O   ⊿ ●●
12
11 O   ⊿ ●●
10
9   ●●
8
7 ⊿ O   ●●
6
5 ⊿   O ●●
4
3 ⊾ O ●●
2
1   ●●

Multiple of 8 sts plus 2.

198

199

200

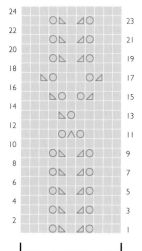

```
24                            23
22          O⅃  ⅃O            21
20          O⅃  ⅃O            19
18          O⅃  ⅃O            17
16        ⅃O      O⅃          15
14        ⅃O      O⅃          13
12          ⅃O              11
10        O∧O
 8          O⅃  ⅃O            9
 6          O⅃  ⅃O            7
 4          O⅃  ⅃O            5
 2          O⅃  ⅃O            3
            O⅃  ⅃O            1
```

Multiple of 11 sts.

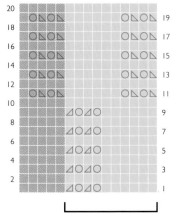

```
20  O⅃O⅃        O⅃O⅃  19
18  O⅃O⅃        O⅃O⅃  17
16  O⅃O⅃        O⅃O⅃  15
14  O⅃O⅃        O⅃O⅃  13
12  O⅃O⅃        O⅃O⅃  11
10          ⅃O⅃O          9
 8          ⅃O⅃O          7
 6          ⅃O⅃O          5
 4          ⅃O⅃O          3
 2          ⅃O⅃O          1
```

Multiple of 10 sts plus 5.

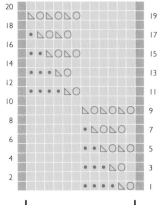

```
20  ⅃O⅃O⅃O              19
18  • ⅃O⅃O              17
16  • • ⅃O⅃O            15
14  • • • ⅃O            13
12  • • • • ⅃O          11
10                ⅃O⅃O⅃O    9
 8              • ⅃O⅃O      7
 6            • • ⅃O⅃O      5
 4          • • • ⅃O        3
 2        • • • • ⅃O        1
```

Multiple of 12 sts plus 2.

201

Panel of 9 sts.

202

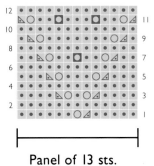

Panel of 13 sts.

▣

(K1, p1, k1, p1, k1) in st to make 5 sts from 1, turn, k5, turn, pass 2nd, 3rd, 4th and 5th sts over 1st st, k in back of this st.

203

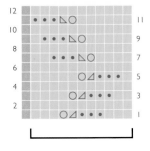

Multiple of 11 sts plus 1.

204

Multiple of 9 sts plus 1.

Panel of 17 sts.

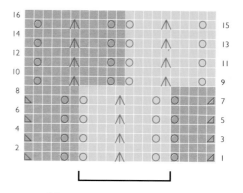

Multiple of 10 sts plus 11.

207

208

Multiple of 10 sts plus 7.

Multiple of 12 sts plus 7.

209

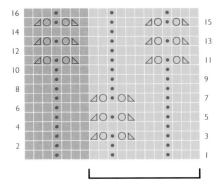

Motif of 17 sts.

210

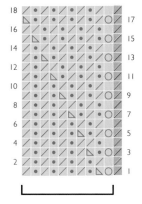

Multiple of 10 sts plus 1.

K2 tog *through back of loops.*

211

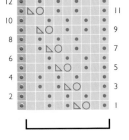

Multiple of 9 sts plus 1.

212

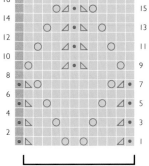

Multiple of 12 sts plus 1.

213

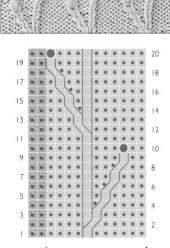

Multiple of 11 sts plus 2.

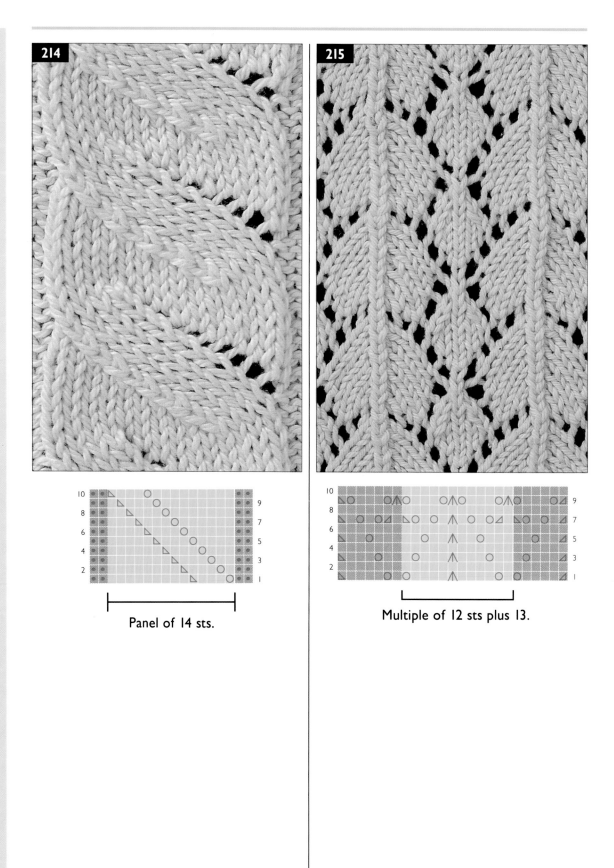

Panel of 14 sts.

Multiple of 12 sts plus 13.

216

217

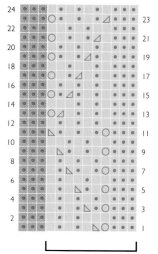

Multiple of 10 sts plus 3.

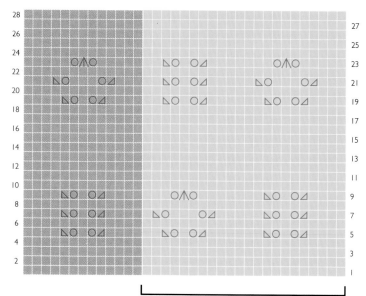

Multiple of 22 sts plus 13.

LACE AND BOBBLE STITCHES

218

219

Multiple of 16 sts plus 1.

Multiple of 10 sts plus 13.

220

Panel of 17 sts.

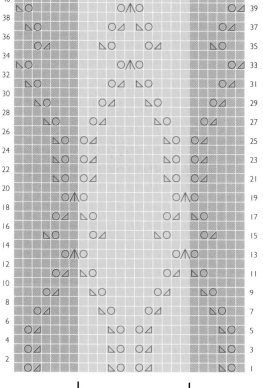

221

222

Multiple of 12 sts plus 13.

Panel of 19 sts.

223

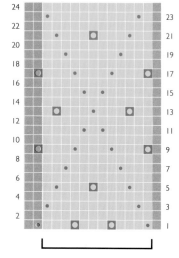

Multiple of 12 sts plus 3.

224

Multiple of 16 sts plus 17.

225

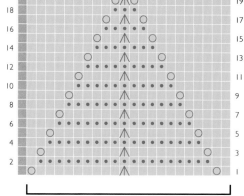

Multiple of 22 sts plus 1.

226

227

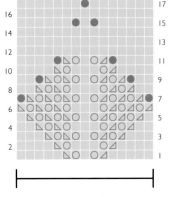

Motif of 15 sts.

Multiple of 16 sts plus 17.

228

Motif of 16 sts.

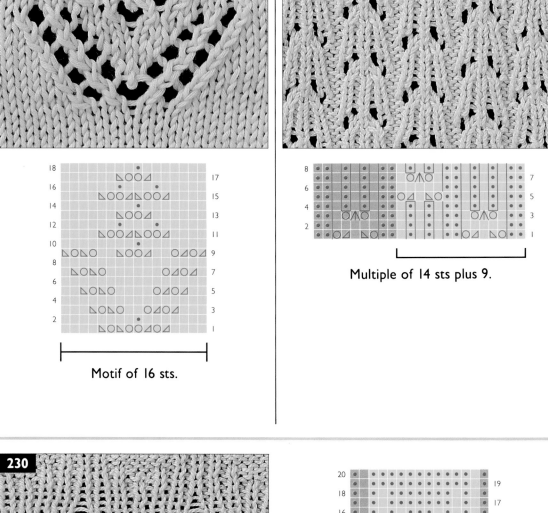

229

Multiple of 14 sts plus 9.

230

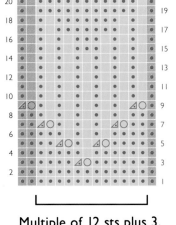

Multiple of 12 sts plus 3.

231

232

Panel of 16 sts.

Panel of 17 sts.

233

24		◿◣	●		○ ○	
22		◿◣	●		○ ○	23
20		◿◣	●		○ ○	21
18		◿◣	●		○ ○	19
16		◿◣	●		○ ○	17
14		◿◣	●		○ ○	15
12						13
10		○ ○	●	◿◣		11
8		○ ○	●	◿◣		9
6		○ ○	●	◿◣		7
4		○ ○	●	◿◣		5
2		○ ○	●	◿◣		3
						1

Multiple of 12 sts plus 4.

234

Multiple of 12 sts plus 13.

235

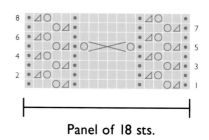

Panel of 18 sts.

◥◤◢◣ Sl next 3 sts on to right-hand needle, k in front and back of next st, k2, pass 3 slipped sts over 4 sts just worked.

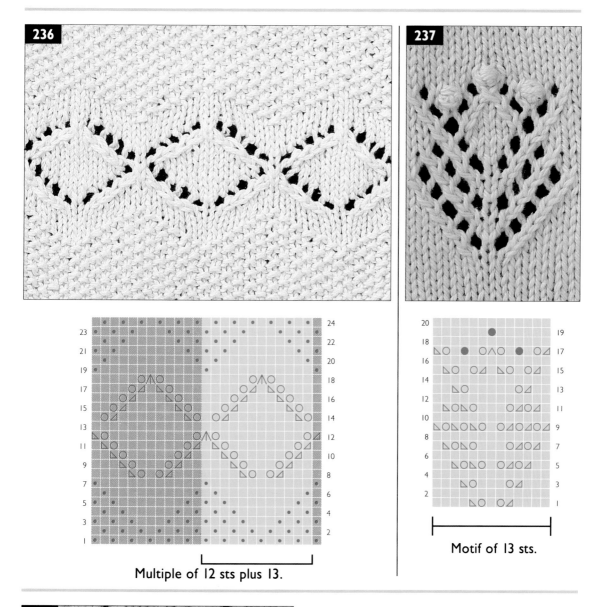

236

Multiple of 12 sts plus 13.

237

Motif of 13 sts.

238

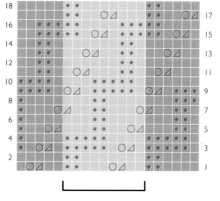

Multiple of 9 sts plus 11.

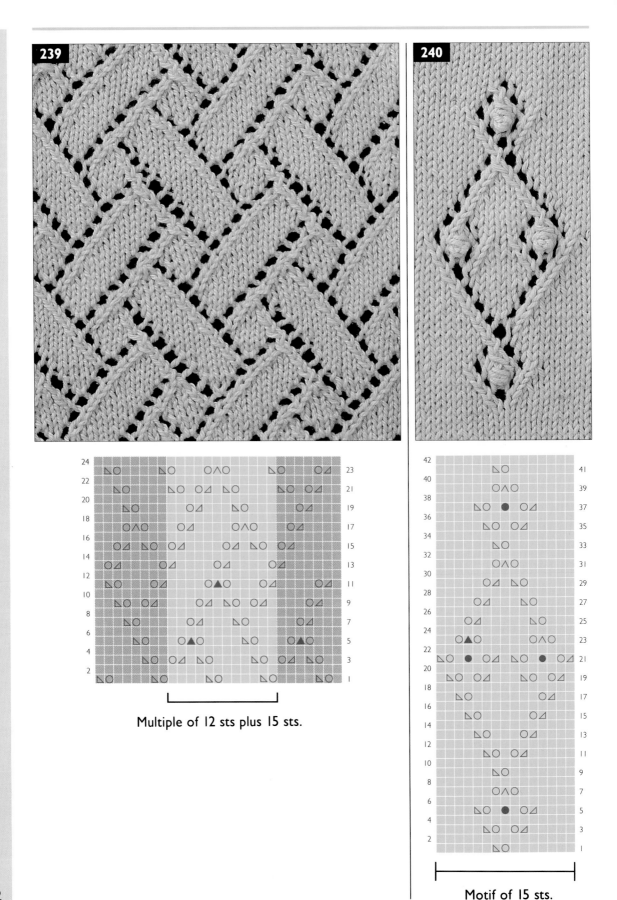

239

24													

Multiple of 12 sts plus 15 sts.

240

Motif of 15 sts.

241

Panel of 7 sts.

242

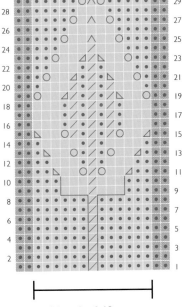

Motif of 13 sts.

243

244

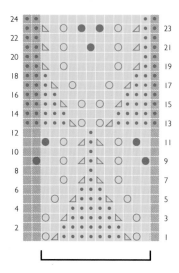

Multiple of 12 sts plus 3.

Multiple of 16 sts plus 9.

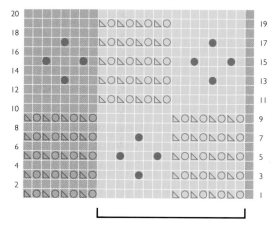

(K1, p1, k1, p1, k1, p1, k1) in st
to make 7 sts from 1, pass
2nd, 3rd, 4th, 5th, 6th and
7th sts, one at a time, over
1st st.

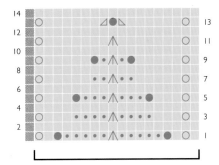

245

246

Panel of 23 sts.

Multiple of 18 sts plus 1.

247

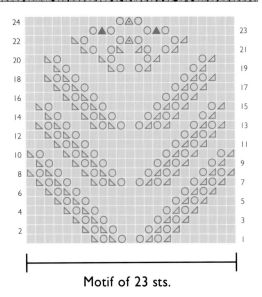

Motif of 23 sts.

248

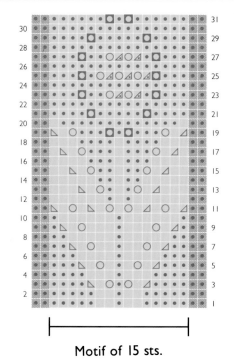

Motif of 15 sts.

249

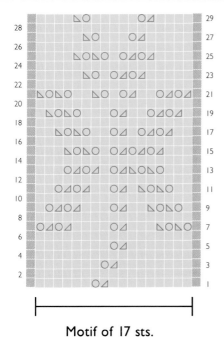

Motif of 17 sts.

250

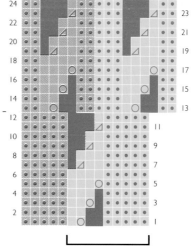

Multiple of 6 sts plus 5.

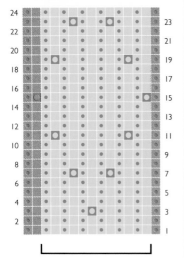

Multiple of 12 sts plus 3.

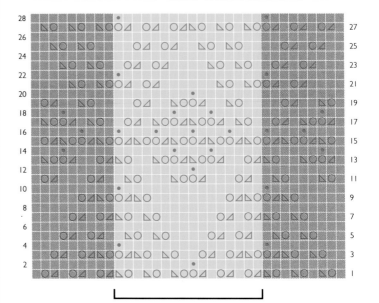

Multiple of 16 sts plus 18.

253

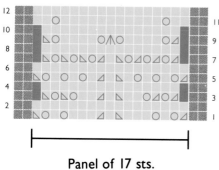

Panel of 17 sts.

254

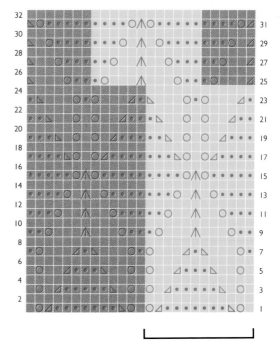

Multiple of 12 sts plus 13.

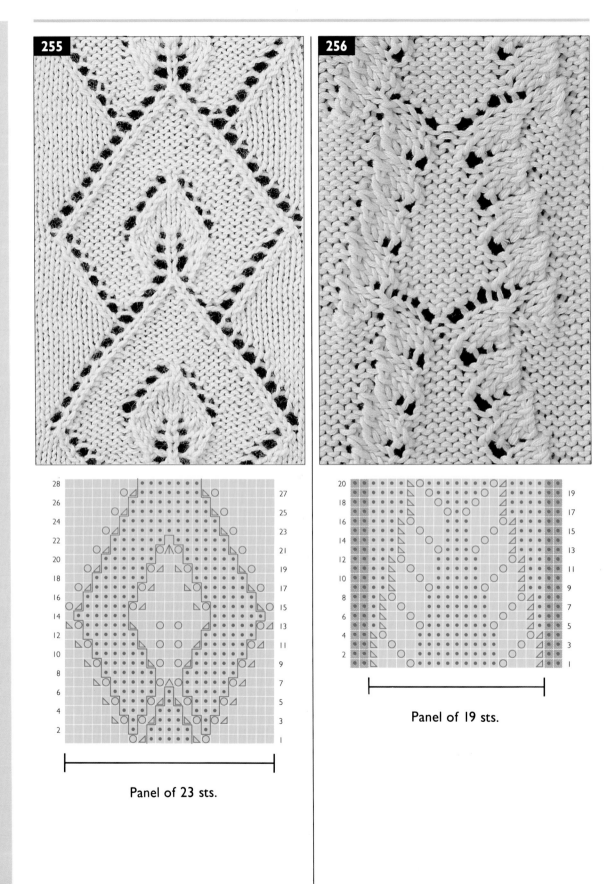

255

256

Panel of 23 sts.

Panel of 19 sts.

Panel of 17 sts.

257

258

259

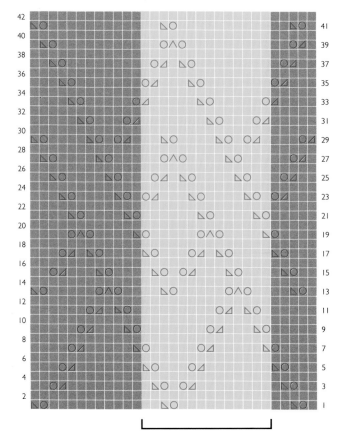

Panel of 2 sts.

Multiple of 14 sts plus 17.

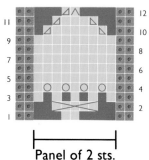

Sl 1 st on to cable needle
and hold at front, [k1, yo]
twice in next st then k1 st
from cable needle.

260

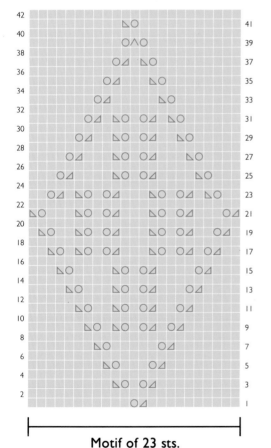

Motif of 23 sts.

261

Motif of 17 sts.

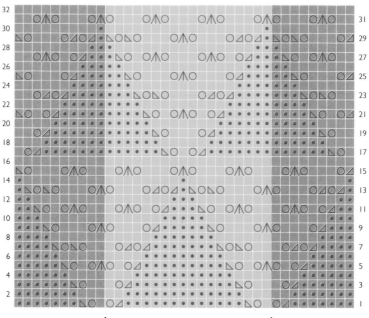

Multiple of 18 sts plus 19.

263

264

Motif of 13 sts.

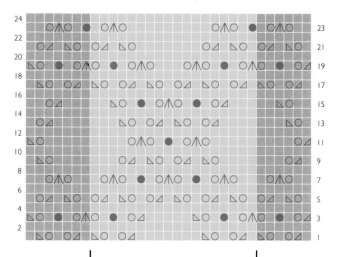

Multiple of 18 sts plus 13.

265

Panel of 37 sts.

266

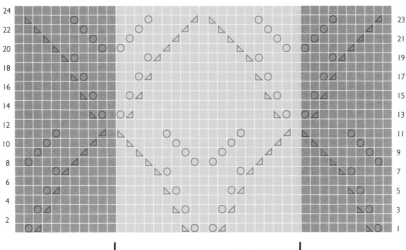

Multiple of 20 sts plus 21.

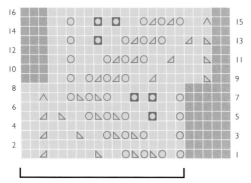

Multiple of 18 sts plus 5.

Motif of 17 sts.

269

270

Motif of 8 sts.

Panel of 26 sts.

271

272

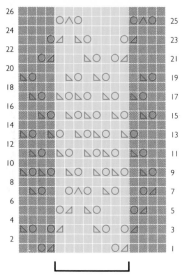

Multiple of 8 sts plus 8.

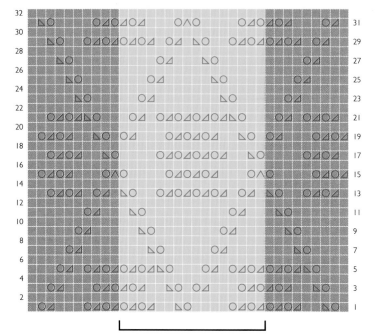

Multiple of 16 sts plus 19.

273

274

Multiple of 16 sts plus 19.

Panel of 13 sts.

275

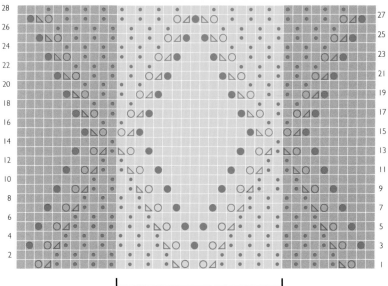

Multiple of 18 sts plus 21.

Multiple of 6 sts plus 6.

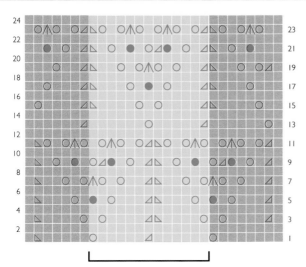

Multiple of 13 sts plus 15.

278

Cast on 6 sts.

279

Cast on 11 sts.

280

Cast on 7 sts.

281

Cast on 6 sts.

282

Cast on 19 sts.

283

Cast on 5 sts.

284

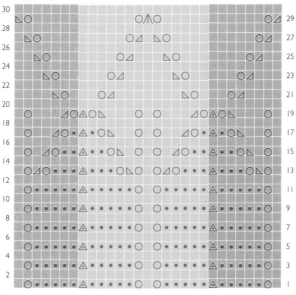

Multiple of 14 sts plus 15.

285

286

Cast on 10 sts.

Cast on 10 sts.

287

288

Cast on 15 sts.

Cast on 12 sts.

Cast on 32 sts.

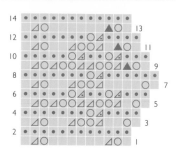

Cast on 12 sts.

291

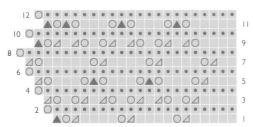

Cast on 22 sts.

292

Cast on 7 sts.

293

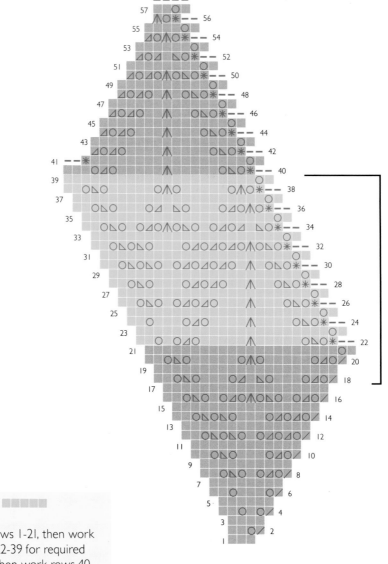

Work rows 1-21, then work rows 22-39 for required length, then work rows 40-57, cast off remaining 4 sts.

Cast on 3 sts.

Motif of 31 sts.

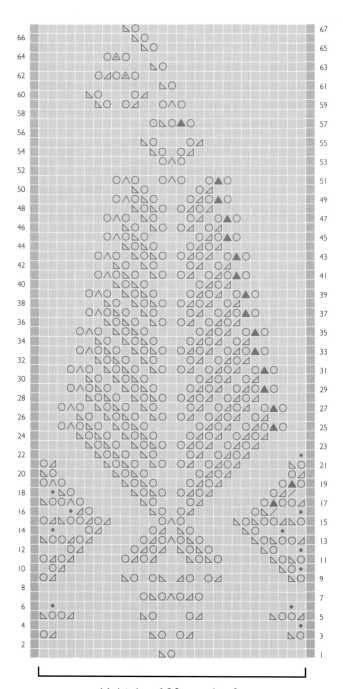

Multiple of 29 sts plus 2.

TWIST AND OTHER STITCHES

Twisting two stitches by working the second before the first gives a similar appearance to a one-over-one cable but has the advantage that a cable needle isn't required and so large areas of twist stitches can be worked where it would be tedious to cable. Although not quite as well-defined as cables, twist stitches give a linear, raised texture to the surface of the knitting and also contract the fabric. This can be compensated for by working increases below and decreases above the twist stitch areas, or stitches such as eyelets can be used to open up the fabric.

Another method of embossing is to work multiple increases which raise the surface of the knitting. The shapes which result can be designed to look like leaves and fruit and so extend the possibilities of making pictures without using colour.

296

Multiple of 6 sts plus 3.
This stitch is reversible.

297

Multiple of 8 sts plus 1.

298

Multiple of 5 sts plus 4.

299

Multiple of 7 sts.

300

Multiple of 4 sts plus 3.

301

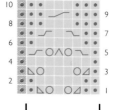

Multiple of 8 sts plus 1.

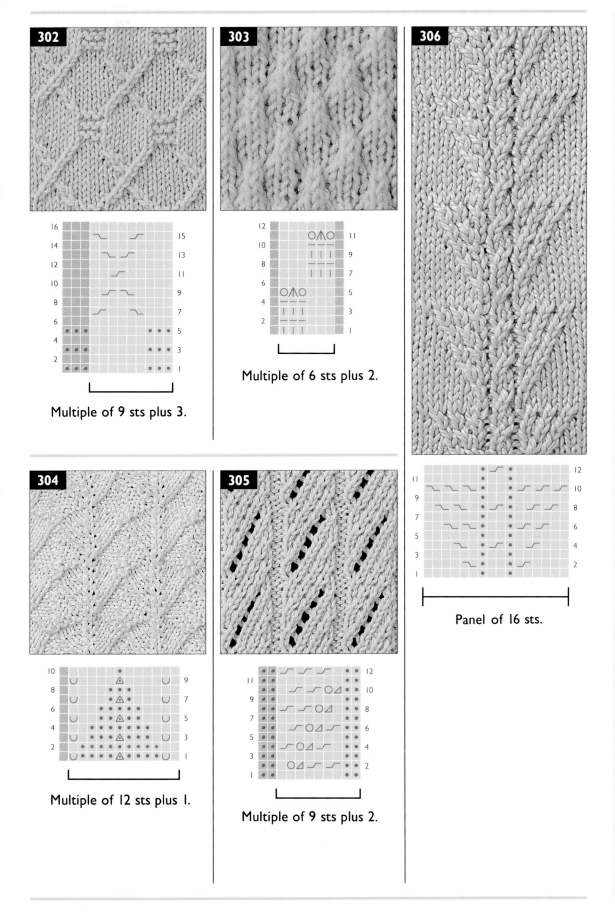

302

Multiple of 9 sts plus 3.

303

Multiple of 6 sts plus 2.

306

Panel of 16 sts.

304

Multiple of 12 sts plus 1.

305

Multiple of 9 sts plus 2.

307

Multiple of 10 sts.

(K1, p1, k1, p1, k1) in st to make 5 sts from 1.

K5 on RS rows, p5 on WS rows.

▲

P5 tog.

308

Multiple of 12 sts plus 6.

309

Multiple of 13 sts plus 7.

310

311

312

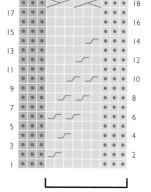

Multiple of 9 sts plus 3.

Multiple of 10 sts.

Multiple of 10 sts plus 2.

313

Multiple of 8 sts plus 1.
(Note that rows 9-16 are a
multiple of 4 sts plus 5.)

179

Panel of 28 sts.

Panel of 10 sts.

316

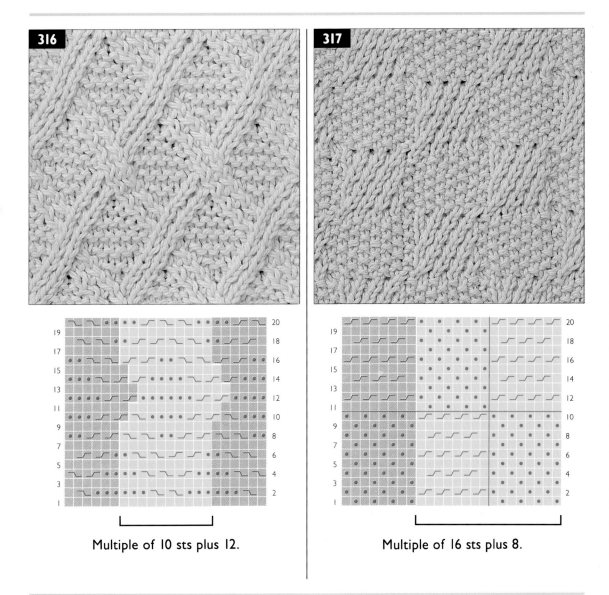

Multiple of 10 sts plus 12.

317

Multiple of 16 sts plus 8.

318

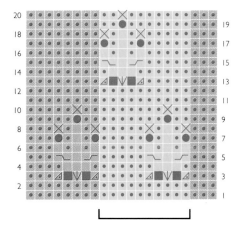

Multiple of 10 sts plus 11.

319

Multiple of 10 sts plus 2.

320

Multiple of 10 sts plus 6.

323

Multiple of 9 sts.

321

Multiple of 12 sts.

322

Multiple of 12 sts plus 3.

324

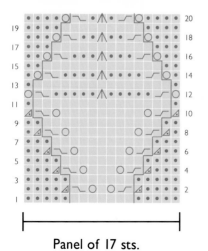

Panel of 17 sts.

325

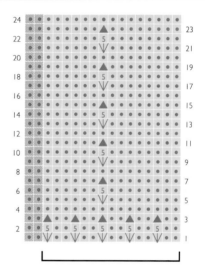

Multiple of 15 sts plus 2.

∨∨

(P1, k1, p1, k1, p1) in st to
make 5 sts from 1.

5

K5.

▲

With yarn at back, sl 4 sts
purlwise, p1, take 4 slipped
sts over p1.

326

Multiple of 10 sts plus 2.

327

Motif of 19 sts.

328

329

Motif of 34 sts.

Multiple of 12 sts.

330

Panel of 11 sts.

331

Multiple of 28 sts plus 32.

Chart A

Chart A is worked first and is a motif of 54 sts, decreased to 53 sts on row 39. Chart B is then worked consecutively, the motif starting with 53 sts on row 41. The stitch count then varies until 53 sts are resumed on row 106.

332

Chart B